Out of Iona

Out of Iona

Words from a crossroads of the world

Jan Sutch Pickard

WILD GOOSE PUBLICATIONS

Copyright © Jan Sutch Pickard, 2003

First published 2003 by
Wild Goose Publications
Fourth Floor, Savoy House, 140 Sauchiehall Street, Glasgow G2 3DH, UK
web: www.ionabooks.com
Wild Goose Publications is the publishing division of the Iona Community.
Scottish Charity No. SCO03794. Limited Company Reg. No. SCO96243.

ISBN 1 901557 77 4

Cover batik illustration © Anna Pickard

A catalogue record for this book is available from the British Library.

Overseas distribution
Australia: Willow Connection Pty Ltd, Unit 4A, 3-9 Kenneth Road, Manly Vale, NSW 2093
New Zealand: Pleroma, Higginson Street, Otane 4170, Central Hawkes Bay
Canada: Novalis Publishing & Distribution, 49 Front Street East, Toronto, Ontario M5E 1B3

Permission to reproduce any part of this work in Australia or New Zealand should be sought from Willow Connection.

Printed by Cromwell Press, Trowbridge, Wiltshire, UK.

Contents

Foreword

These last nine years or so we in the Iona Community, and many others, have been richly blessed by three successive Iona Wardens whose experience, insights and creativity have been expressed, and thus shared more widely, through their writing. Peter Millar (Warden from 1995–98) produced *Iona – a pilgrim guide* in 1997 and *An Iona prayer book* in 1998, which he has followed up with further books – *Waymarks* (2000) and *Finding Hope Again* (2003). Brian Woodcock (Warden 1998–2001), together with members of the resident staff group who were working at the Community's islands centres at the time, compiled the latest edition (2001) of the *Iona Abbey Worship Book* and wrote, with Jan Sutch Pickard, *Advent Readings from Iona*. And now Jan herself, who has been Warden since 2001, has collected some of her recent poems, reflections and worship material in *Out of Iona*.

As the Community's Leader from 1995 until 2002 it was my privilege and joy to work with these gifted people, my friends – to accompany, learn from, and try to support them

– and, ever so occasionally, 'manage' them! The Warden's task is immensely demanding: the Community's islands work is our 'shop window': along with the activities of the Wild Goose Resource Group in the field of worship and all the material that Wild Goose Publications produces, it is our major 'public face'. Many people are surprised to discover that the Community's administrative headquarters are in Glasgow, where almost as many staff are based as on Iona, and that the Community's members do not live on Iona but are dispersed throughout Britain, and a few beyond, living out their commitment to the Community's purpose and concerns in a wide variety of local situations.

But it is to Iona that the Community continues to look for so much of our nourishment and inspiration; it is to Iona that we keep going back; and it is to Iona that countless others come whether as day visitors or holidaymakers, as guests to share for almost a week in the 'common life' experience at the Community's islands centres (the restored Benedictine Abbey, and the MacLeod Centre built in 1998), or as resident staff members or volunteers (150 or so a year from all over the world) contributing to the ministry of hospitality through the work of the centres. And it is the Warden's task somehow to hold this all together, to develop co-operative and participative ways of working, to be creative in exercising overall responsibility for daily worship and sensitive in responding to the pastoral demands, to be an 'ambassador' on Iona on behalf of the Community. It is something of a miracle that Jan, like Peter and Brian before her, in the face of all this, has found the time to write as well!

But, as Jan makes very clear, the writing comes out of the daily experience, much of it in moments snatched out of the hectic rush or added on at the start or end of the day. Indeed Iona, at least around the village and our centres, is not really such a peaceful place as some imagine. One of our staff members once said famously, 'People come to Iona looking for peace and quiet and they go away looking for peace and justice!' A former Deputy Leader of the Community, Ralph Morton, who worked with George MacLeod, the Community's Founder and Leader, for many years, said, 'The Iona experience is for export.' Many of those who come to Iona are on a spiritual pilgrimage, seeking to make sense of life, looking for opportunities to explore, learn and grow, reflecting on the significance and relevance of faith to the challenges and pressures of life.

Within the Iona Community we believe that spirituality is about engagement not escape – engaging with God in the midst of life, in creation, in relationships, in the struggles and issues of today's world. So, as George MacLeod said again and again in so many different ways, God is to be discovered and experienced in 'every blessed thing'; and what really matters is what we do, once we get back home, with the insights and experiences we have had on Iona.

The wonderful breadth and depth of Jan's writing here will come as no surprise to those who are familiar with *Vice Versa*, the collection of prayers, poems and reflections that she published after being Vice-President of the Methodist Conference of Great Britain in 1996–97, or, for example, with her contributions to *Dandelions and Thistles* (1998 – which she edited) and *The One Loaf* (2000 – edited by Joy Mead). Jan writes with verve and energy. She is a great 'story-teller' and has an enviable way with words: you can see the people, feel the emotions, so easily imagine yourself into the situations she is writing about. Her sharpness of insight and her own compassionate, cheerful, supportive personality are evident on every page. Shut your eyes and you can so easily hear her reading the poems, sharing the reflections, leading the prayers in the Abbey church or in a gathering in the chapter-house or MacLeod Centre community room. For the great thing is that these writings of Jan's have not been composed in abstract detachment from where the action is: they are thoroughly grounded in the hurly-burly of life on Iona; every telling phrase and vivid image comes out of the experience of the daily round of demanding tasks in their amazing variety – from the mundane down-to-earth routine chores to the emergencies and challenges that stretch you to the limit of your resources; covering the whole gamut of emotions from deep pain, sadness and bitterness to the joy and laughter that soars and sings.

And through it all Jan's own convictions and commitment shine ever so clearly – a faith that engages with everyday realities, explores, struggles, asks the hard questions, yet is ultimately unshakable. This is a book in which, with its evocation of life on Iona and its sheer artistry, I know that many will find inspiration and enjoyment.

Norman Shanks
Govan Old Parish Church, Glasgow
September 2003

Out of Iona

Take us outside, O Christ, outside holiness,
out to where soldiers curse and nations clash
at the crossroads of the world.
So shall this building continue to be justified.

(From a prayer by George MacLeod, used in the Iona Community daily Office)

Introduction

Iona is a place of paradoxes. You may well have bought this book because the name of a small Hebridean island appears in its title. It may have been a place of pilgrimage for you, as for many others. It is a place where many people come, and are moved by its beauty; but they are changed and challenged too. The first poem, *Iona Weaving*, attempts to describe this complexity. Make no mistake, that poem was not written (any more than this introduction) in a serene moment on the sea shore or at leisure in the Abbey library – but hammered out on a worn keyboard, at a desk piled with papers, late at night and between meetings, as a liturgy for use among folk living through a time of tiredness, change and loss. It is about both the pressures of life here, on a small island – in the busy life of the season and the powerful isolation of the winter – and the blessings.

All the material here comes 'out of Iona': it was written, inspired, developed or used here: in the Abbey church and the Iona Community's centres, in conversations with island neighbours. That is the unifying factor. I have divided it into sections which seem to me to make sense. First there are *poems*, written over several years, some quirky and secular, some marking stages on my faith journey (though not necessarily orthodox statements of belief), some which were subsequently shared in acts of worship, some written for friends.

Then, the largest section is *biblical reflections*, written with a very particular purpose, as part of the Ministry of the Word in services, for instance the Prayers for Healing held every Tuesday in the Abbey. At the end of this book there is an appendix about ways of using these reflections. It is not exhaustive, but draws on what worked in the original service – a kind of 'serving suggestion'.

At the end are three *sequences* which take us 'out of Iona'. The longest piece, 'Thembi's House', is about a Habitat for Humanity project in South Africa, in which I took part just before coming to work on Iona. In a sense that particular and chosen experience – of an amazing mixture of folk working together, finding common ground, building community – has been part of the fabric of my life on Iona; just as songs from South Africa are woven into our worship. A book with nothing but the landscapes and moods and associations of this island could be beautiful but claustrophobic. Iona is not only a unique and welcoming place; it is and always has been a sending place. These final, longer, poems are about going away, which is part of the pilgrimage for each of us, back into a wider world: of city streets, hospital wards, police stations and a developing world where community still needs to be built. Here prayer and politics belong together just as much as they do on Iona, but we may be called to engage in a different way – as I discovered when, in the same year, I set off on a sabbatical journey full of questions; found myself suddenly helpless in hospital; and at another point chose to step into the road to sit down outside the nuclear submarine base at Faslane. It was out of my experience on Iona that I found the courage to do each of these things.

So the book ends with the experience we all share, of leaving the island and continuing on our journey, in the world and with God.

Jan Sutch Pickard
Iona, Lent 2003

Words from a small island

– Poems –

Iona weaving

How can we comprehend it, God,
this beauty and this pain?
How does it hold together?
Is there pattern or purpose?

On a still December day,
warp and weft glimpsed
in the gold threads of the dawn sky,
in the blue-grey restless waters of the Sound,
in our laughter and our tears,
in our life together in this place –
your mysterious weaving of the world.

In the battle-song and surge of the waves
        and the living silence of the hills.
In the welter of winter gales
        and the sheltering space of church or home.
In angry exchanges that unravel,
        and words and spaces that heal.
In isolation and in solitude.
In welcomes at the jetty
        and in saying goodbye.
In the wind-bent trees, blasted by salt
        and flowers flourishing in the village gardens.
In busyness that leaves no time
        and folk making time, here and now.
In the richness of all we are given
        in the ache of all we have lost.
In discord –
        and in ceilidh music.
Stumbling in the dark –
        and dancing under the stars.

How can we comprehend it:
Your beauty and ours – who are made in your image?

Our pain and yours – who chose to share our lives?
We cannot hold it together – but it holds us.

Help us to see pattern and purpose,
    and our part
in the weaving of the world.
Amen

*(This was written in part as a blessing of Mhairi Killin's artwork
Iona Weave, 13.12.2001)*

Iona weaving

The curve

The curve
of this wave,
rolling toward the shore
in a westerly gale,
growing to its full height
and breaking into white blossom
along its leaf-green, glass-green,
greenstone, scythe-sharp edge –
the curve
of the wave

and the curved petals
of a single snowdrop
(sheltering from the wind)
draw on the same energy,
flowing from a Creator
who signs every work in freehand,
with a flourish,
delights
in detail

and is here and now

watching the wave,
holding the snowdrop
in a cupped hand –
God of power and pity.

Anemones

Easy to see things in black and white;
challenging to make moves across the chequered board.
But consider these flowers,
which are not concerned with winning or losing,
spin no journalistic yarns,
are not doing but being;
purple for royalty and mourning,
red for blood,
colours of God's laughter and tears
and of our hunger for living.

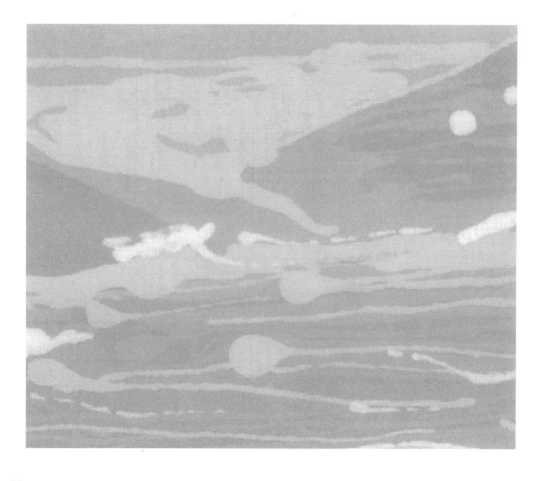

Tooth

None of these peaks is missing:
arrayed round the horizon
like teeth felt with a tongue,
reassuring and always strange,
rounded, smooth, jagged – familiarly
they greet the ferry
as she slips from harbour –
are not the end but the background,
the context of the journey.
They are there.

One of my wisdom teeth is gone:
I feel the gap.
My tongue returns, tenderly,
missing its solidity, its size –
a small thing, but my own.
Bit by bit I am being worn away,
as mountains by millennia.

It takes less time for human beings –
three score years and ten –
though family history remembers
great uncle Peter, sand-grounder,
eating the fish he caught daily,
and still with all his own teeth at eighty.

Even now I've a reasonable showing
for a crust of new-baked bread,
an apple, a smile.
But behind the smile,
in the secret places my tongue knows,
there is less. This is not the end –
the journey continues –
but the horizons are changing:
one of these peaks is missing.

Riddle

It moves mountains
of green water
marbled with white
   and is a playground
   for the seabirds.
It shakes stone buildings
to their foundations
   and teases sheep –
   carding their wool the wrong way.
It howls outside shut doors,
worries flocks of clouds,
   sings hymns in the rafters
   of churches built to keep it out –
and leaves preachers and poets
out of breath, wordless.

Ruben

Your gift is silence
watchfulness, a shy smile
a listening presence,
a discipline of learning –
silence is your gift.

What is your story?
A drawn breath,
a handful of words,
a glimpse of a far place,
a different life.

You live in the present,
exploring with delight
the history of this place –
shards becoming treasure
as you tell the story with wonder –
through you the stones speak.

The real gold is your joy in it all:
your passionate pilgrimage,
writing hundreds of words
to hand on, to all who have ears to hear,
all you have learned,
all you now understand.

But at our last meal together,
amid convivial clamour,
words are not enough:
your voice falters
you start to speak, fall silent

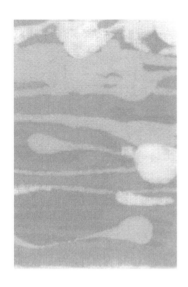

and in response
silence spreads among us
like rings on water –
we too are lost for words.

Your meaning reaches the depths
of our being – without needing words –
we are rocked in its wake,
changed for ever by your presence.

Your gift is silence.

Ruben

Mary Magdalene

*(for Hendrikje,
who modelled her in clay)*

She is a strong woman
with strong hands –
but now they are empty
spread out
helplessly
to the hungry sky.

She is a living being
but frozen in time –
going nowhere –
gaunt as a dead tree
gazing
up at the chaotic sky.

She is a strong woman –
her unique beauty
made terrible by grief –
her mouth opens, wordless
questioning
the empty sky.

She is a strong woman
and yet she weeps.

Being there

(for Jane)

Daisies,
looking the sun straight in the eye;
time
to talk and listen, to laugh and cry;
a place
to be human together;
celandines,
paving the way with pure gold;
a cup
offered in welcome;
acceptance –
simple and needed, like water to quench thirst;
a garden
of sea-worn stones, each with its own story;
a lark,
whose song shimmers in the sky –
small ordinary bird, barely seen
celebrating God in the everyday;

honest words

shared silences

an open door.

Dun Bhuirg

This place smells of sheep –
a noost on the crag-top,
dungy, lined with wool.
Once it smelled of human beings,
huddling together under a low roof,
between walls they had built
against the common enemies
of wind, rain and darkness.

Leaving behind few traces
of their daily life
in this fortress of ordinary folk;
traces of fire, a stone scraper,
a broken string of beads.

Some things barely change:
old field patterns, distant islands,
waves' litany below,
tormentil starring the turf,
gulls' arc against the sun.

But their words, these far folk,
their songs and stories, faith and fears,
and their names, are lost for ever –
wiped from the world's memory
as the waves below Dun Bhuirg flow
and ebb, leaving the sand a blank.

Gary

He is walking backwards –
Gary
a small child
with a surprised shock of hair
and a nine-year-old
wonder at the world,
determined
to explore it on his own terms –
walking backwards.

Returning from the shore,
slowly
savouring each moment:
a new-born calf on the croft,
song and smell of the sea,
a crab's claw, a skipped stone
shared laughter
and the sun chasing the rain ...
with a pocketful of shells,
with wave-filled wellies –
walking backwards.

What lies ahead?
Can he help
walking into the sky-darkening squall
of parents' anger?
Where does it leave him –
the violence
of confused and confusing people
confronting death with denial?

Gary,
gazing down the road,
remembering his day,
sees a rainbow over the far shore –
and goes on walking
                backwards.

Genesis 1 & 2: Iona

Today I glimpse chaos:
clouds swirling down the mountains,
waves running before the wind,
gusts battering our walls;
ferries cancelled, plans banjaxed.

Today I glimpse God at work:
moving on the waters,
brooding on the abyss,
breathing life into our clay –
creating new possibilities: seeing the good.

Today I get down to work:
out of chaos imagining God.

Knowing my place in creation,
I begin to name what I see.

Winter wings

Just below Sithean,
(Fairy Hill becoming Hill of the Angels)
standing water has turned into ice.
Not an opaque skim
on a muddy puddle,
but complete transformation.

Now, unfolding across the winter grass,
intricate crystals, spars, fractals,
fragile panes patterned with leaves and feathers.

Opening up new possibilities –
like growing things,

like spread wings.

Midwinter poems

(for Neil)

1. The shortest day

This is the shortest day.
A shy sun hugs the horizon;
life is at a low ebb,
wrack piled on the shore,
waves making a litany of endings,
sap shrinking in bare branches –
intricate but barren against the sky –
signs of life clenched in the corm.

This is the shortest day.
From now on there is more light
day by day; brace yourself for more cold,
but the coming snow will make a clean end,
and prepare the ground for new beginnings.
Under earth, snowdrop and crocus
are coiled like springs.
This is the shortest day –
from now on it gets better.

2. Snow colours

A day full of colour
in spite of snow – or because of it.
Golden bands in the dawn sky
overcome by a second darkness,
dense grey matted like sheep's wool,
falling flakes, veiling a leaden sea
red
of a robin's breast –
a small bird in a huge and alien territory –
green of a leaf surprised to be alive,
yellow of a jacket on the hill where people at play
whoop and slither and scramble up,
against clouds gathering
purple like a new bruise.

Sea becoming steel, becoming bronze with verdigris.
Gold of withies wick with new life.
Ice blue of the distant hills and sky:
a dusting of sunlight on one, like pollen.
Orange peel of a Christmas treat, tossed aside,
rose pink of high clouds, catching the sunset,
indigo of the night drawing on.
Such eloquent colour
in a white and silent world, cold but not dead:
like a sheet of paper
waiting to be written.

3. Snow dog
Fingal
first-foots a field
chasing birds – printing delight
in black and white.

4. Blessing for a poet
Your poem
is not simply about the words you choose
or even the words that choose you.
It is about being
the way you are –
sometimes without rhyme or reason
but always with integrity and passion.
May the Maker bless
all you are making of your life,
as you discover that of God in you.

Midwinter poems

Millennium

For millennia
the light of the stars has travelled.
For a thousand years
this cross has withstood the winds.
For a hundred years of war
wave has followed wave
while people walking in darkness
have longed for peace.
But before our time, before all time:
in the beginning, the Word.

In this moment
the snowflake, a perfect crystal,
is formed and falls.
In this moment
the snowdrop, in the dark earth,
waits for the returning sun.
In this moment
a child is born,
a life begins, blooms.
And in this time, our time, God's time:
in each beginning, the Word.

Another day

(for Anna)

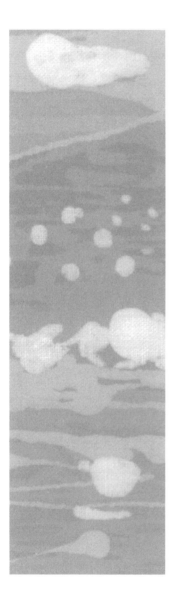

Another day –
a day that God has made –
the sky is mother-of-pearl
like the inside of a sea shell;
the sea is moving darkness
and then dancing with light
as the sun rises over Mull.
Every stone has its own shadow,
every blade of grass is shining.
Alarm clocks go off,
feet hit the floor,
porridge is on the stove,
bells ring,
feet are on the stairs,
toast smells good,
folk gather,
grace is said,
a hundred cups of tea are poured,
the sun climbs the sky
and the big bell rings for worship.
Feet are on the road.
Now the world is on the move,
wheels are turning,
ships putting out to sea,
cows coming to the milking,
shops opening,
a catch being landed,
computers being switched on,
school bells ringing.

On the far side of Mull
bus engines start up,
wheels begin to turn.
As the sun travels across the sky,
folk travel toward Iona,
to the ferry:
the day visitors, tourists, trippers,
pilgrims on their way
at the beginning of the day –
the day that God has made.

Story

You must go to the end of the road
and then beyond.
There are ten houses by the harbour,
wading birds, an embedded anchor,
but the boats have all gone.
Further on, heading north
between two hills,
walk where the grass is tawny –
beware the emerald green –
and you will come to a hillside
tilting toward the restless waves.
Three black birds
are sitting on a rock, biding their time.
There is a seal, too
(but if you watch it will not change).
Islands beckon on the horizon.

Keep your feet on the ground and look closer.
Here find mountain ranges, deep valleys
where may be dragons, dark lakes.
This is where the seventh son
makes his perilous journey;
these rocks were pitched by giants in play;
this pool, reflecting the sky,
is where three heads bobbed up,
wanting to be washed by the maiden.

And here is the enchanted forest,
its trunks gnarled, wind-bent,
roots clinging to the rock,
leaves evergreen, branches intertwined
in patterns you will also find
in stone and bronze and in rare books:
but here they come alive.
This is the enchanted forest.
It is only hand-high,
but if you step into it, you will enter the story.

This may be where you will lose your way
and find yourself.

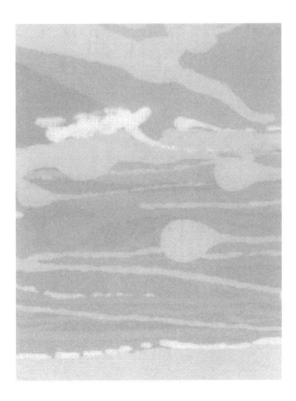

The bird window

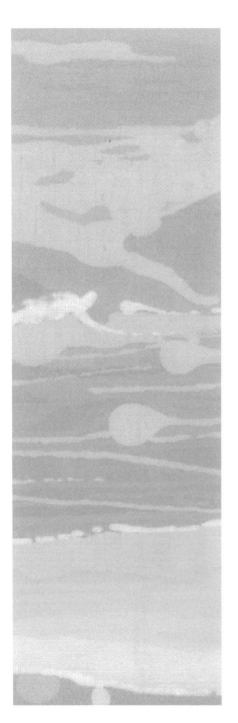

Stone barn
where history is stored
and stories begin.
Folk wandering in
wonder at candlelight and crosslight,
watch dust-motes dance
above the bird-patterned carpet
in sun streaming
through door and window.

But almost out of sight –
high up under the roof –
is one small window.
The first builders made it for birds,
flying into the church,
to find their way out:
for birds seek the highest point of light.

Then, for all the years
the church was in ruins,
cattle sheltered here from the wind
and the sun blessed every corner;
weeds flourished, birds came and went freely
building their nests among the stones –
at home in the holy places.

Reverent rebuilders
put back the lid
and glassed in the bird window,
protecting God's people
from the winds of heaven.
But now any bird, dove or hawk,
trapped in this great structure –
seeking the light but finding
no way out –
could dash itself to death.

If the wings of the Spirit
are beating here,
should we not take the risk
of breaking the glass –
so that she
can fly free,
soar in clear air
and come again among us?

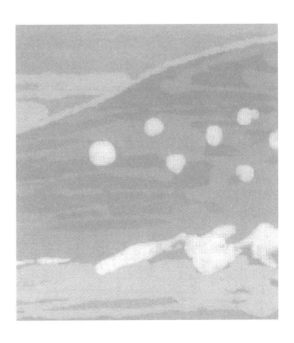

Kingfisher

(for Karen)

Quick! Quick!
Your workmates called –
in the break,
in the one room in the mill
overlooking the river –

Look! Look!
The kingfisher
glimpsed, compact on a branch,
then taking off
across the current –
a flash of lapis lazuli.

Think! Think!
what it was like:
a creature never seen before
coming alive before your eyes
and in your mind.

Look! Look!
Remembered in your words now,
flickering across currents of time –
communicating between the three of us
round a table far from the river –
it still conducts wonder like electricity.

Your kingfisher,
flying in the face of apathy,
banality, the fear of death –
Quick! Quick!

Rainbows do not come cheap

(for Ruth)

Rainbows do not come cheap –
they are born out of the storm.
Crossing grey skies,
they cannot cross them out –
a fragile 'maybe' in the face of doubt.

Rainbows balance on the edge,
in island weather:
a thin tissue of hope spun out
when sun and rain come together.
Sudden, unbidden, glimpsed,
in broken pieces, or a perfect arch.
Coming and going, perverse, diverse …

What is it leaps up
when the dancer can dance no more?
What do children paint and stories celebrate?
What, when horizons and walls close in,
opens an unexpected door?
When the past rises like a tide to drown us
is *terra firma* of the present tense?
When words fail, are beyond words?
Why should a trick of the light
make such a difference?

Rainbows make their own rules:
they make no promises,
but connect imagination and common sense –
follow the logic of God's fools.
Rainbows do not come cheap:
they come to those who weep.

Work gloves

These are my work gloves:
like the hands inside
they have seen better days.
They are crumpled, dusty
and, at points, downright mucky.
They have been stained by paint
and snagged by nails.

But I'm not ashamed of them:
all these are signs of hard work –
after all, I'd rather
wear out than rust away –

and, in their humble way
they help me to see you, God,
at work in the world.

Incarnation is hands-on:
in Jesus you showed yourself ready
to get your hands dirty –
torn by nails, stained red …

These work gloves remind me of your love.

A thin place

Before it fades –
remember, wonder, fumble for words –
what happened the other night?
Aurora Borealis,
the Merry Dancers,
the Northern Lights:

began with a smudge of light –
like a cloud on the dark sky –
as we walked home
on a cold and windy night.
Breathless, we watched the stars fade,
as the cloud, white as wool,
grew and became luminous,
moving minute by minute,
lightness on darkness, unsettling,
shot with subtle iridescence –
whispers of colour …

happening, rose higher in the sky.
I walked out from the shelter of the building,
feeling the full force of the north wind
and then forgetting it,
as I found myself
standing within a great tent,
veils of light billowing down from the zenith
on every side, moving delicately and yet powerfully,
blown by an unearthly wind,
dancing to unheard rhythms.

How long did I stand there
insignificant and blessed,
seeing creation in a new light?

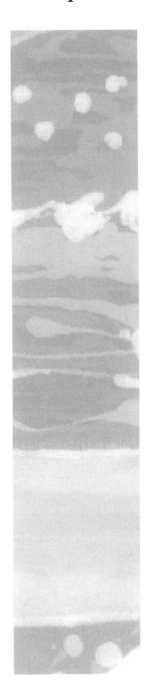

Everything connected.
In a thin place, I stood in God's presence –
knowing myself fully alive –

frozen to the spot
yet dancing to music that will never end.

A thin place

The work of worship

– Biblical reflections –

The Word

In the beginning ...
Silence
(silence)

darkness, void
formless, empty
(silence)

or again
chaos
(random noise)

the big bang
universequakes
rushing mighty winds
(sound behind words)

great balls of fire
primordial soup
out of control
out of order
incoherent
cacophony

meaningless
(silence)

and then
the still small voice
a glimmer of light
pattern
     structure
         dialogue
            meaning
               creation
               (singing bowl)

But in the beginning …
from before the beginning
in the void
underlying the chaos –
the creating Word
(singing bowl)

The Word

Women at the riverside
(Exodus 2:1–11)

A. I am a Levite woman,
    wife of a Levite man.
    I carried his child
    safe in the secret cradle of my womb
    for nine months, afloat
    in the waters of life,
    until the day the waters broke
    and he swam out into a dangerous world.
    For three more months I hid him in our hut,
    but his little voice grew stronger
    so one day I took a basket
    woven of rushes that grow at the water's edge;
    I daubed on tar to make it watertight,
    a little coracle, then took it down,
    to float where the river lapped among the reeds.

B. I am his sister,
    a small solemn child
    standing by the side of a big river,
    to see what will happen.
    I see the river, wide, lazy, slow-moving, life-bearing,
    with the sun glinting on its smooth surface.
    I cannot see our little cradle-boat
    but I know it's there,
    hidden among the whispering reeds,
    with my baby brother.
    I am a big sister, with a huge responsibility.
    I see strangers coming down to the beach
    to play, as though they haven't a care in the world,
    to bathe in the river.
    I see a great lady, one of our enemies.
    Can she see the baby? What will she do?
    My legs turn to water;
    my eyes fill with tears.

C. I am Pharaoh's daughter.
    I left the stale air of the palace,
    the baking courtyards and colonnades,
    the passions of politics,
    the hard facts of life, the reasons of state.
    I walked with my women
    on the bare earth,
    down to where the river offers
    another way of being,
    with its cool flow, its gentle caress, its feelings.
    I wanted freedom to be myself
    in another element,
    and I fell for a baby.

D. I am a slave girl.
    All I did was wade in deep
    and fetch an ordinary basket
    from where it was hidden in the rough reeds.
    Did I guess its secret?
    What did I feel
    as I held it, trembling,
    and heard the hungry cries?
    Who hears my voice?

C. I was moved with pity
    by the tears of the baby.
    I knew it must be a Hebrew child,
    and suddenly, there at my elbow,
    was another child:
    not asking for money
    like your normal urchin, but offering help:
    'Do you want a nurse for the baby?'
    The child has sense – a wise child.
    I suspect there's more in this than meets the eye:

a story I don't know, an alien experience,
a strange and powerful torrent of feeling.
I accepted her help.

B.   I called my mother, like a stranger.

A.   I came and nursed my child, who knew me.

D.   I found him, as lost as myself.

C.   I adopted him, and called him Moses
because I drew him out of the water.

We are the women: a wife
A sister.
A daughter.
A slave –
women without names.

All.   But we are the ones
who trusted the child to the strange and saving waters,
and drew him out alive –
and called him by name.

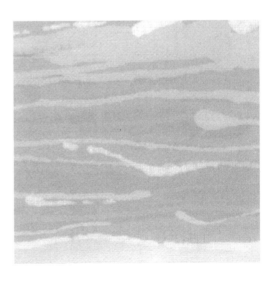

Encounter

(1 KINGS 17:8–16)

Here is a man
on a journey –
needing somewhere to lay his head,
thirsty, hungry.

Here is a woman
on her home ground –
picking up sticks,
wary of strangers.

Both of them are living in a dry land
where a little water, a handful of meal,
need to go a long way.

One has a household to feed;
the other has only himself to keep going
through the wilderness,
until God lets him know why.
He is travelling in faith;
she has given up hope.

A coping woman,
she has now come to the end
of her resources –
just this last ration of meal,
just this trickle of oil,
not much more water,
sticks for a last fire:
just these embers of courage –
she is burnt out.

He is not sure why he is here,
except that God pointed him this way –
to take the food out of the mouths
of this hungry family?
To walk away? Or to watch them die?
What can he do that will change anything?

But she offers him welcome
and he offers encouragement –
and they go on from there.

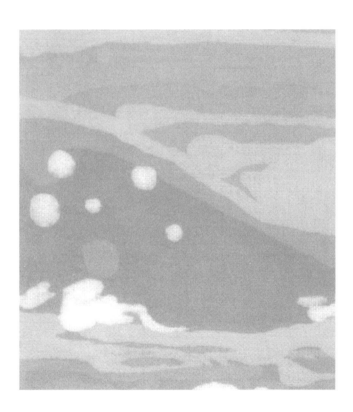

Angels and shepherds

(Luke 2:8–20)

Angels
are experts in communication –
scary how good they are –
that is why they keep on
reassuring mere mortals:
'Do not be afraid.'

Shepherds
are rank amateurs –
lost for words,
stumbling around in the dark:
but fear not, words will be found
for all that needs to be said.

How different we are –
angels and shepherds –
yet part of the same story.
Nothing is wasted,
we are all needed:
all share in God's glory.

The Tempter

(MATT 4:1–4)

I said
'If you are the Son of God
tell these stones to become bread.'
My voice
was the whine of the desert wind:
'If you are the Son of God' …
its dryness whispering over stones,
baking hot,
but hard as disbelief …
'If you are the Son of God
tell these stones' …
madness of empty places,
talking to stones –
'Tell these stones to become bread.'
If they were
then this ache
would be assuaged,
this hollow hunger
would be overcome –
if grey granite and brown sandstone
could become golden-brown,
grainy and fragrant loaves.

Even the word 'bread'
made his mouth water.
He touched them
and set them down, still stones.
'Man cannot live on bread alone
but on every word from the mouth of God.'

I lost that one.
But I left him hungry and alone,
while the wind in the wilderness
whispered over the stones.

Four friends

(Mark 2:1–12)

First friend

They all had their backs to us!
They were trying to see into the house
    where Jesus was talking.
No manners – looking through the windows,
    jammed in the doorway.
Nobody who was inside could get out.
Nobody who was outside could get in.
And as for us, we were complete outsiders.
It made me angry, to see
how our friend was more shut out than anyone else:
couldn't stand up and look over the heads of the crowd;
didn't have the strength to push them away;
couldn't get near enough to hear what Jesus was saying;
just lay there, depending on us.
At least we stood by him.
But the crowds didn't even notice
    whom they were excluding,
because they all had their backs to us …
And I thought, there must be a way through,
so that he's not on the edge
but in the middle where the action is –
where Jesus is.
I don't think Jesus would want anyone to be excluded,
would be angry, if he knew – would raise the roof …
Now there's an idea!

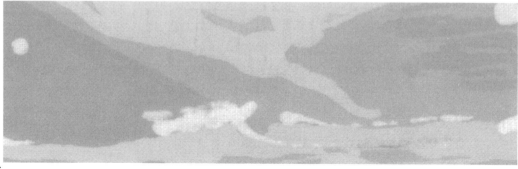

Second friend

It really hurt me to see him that way –
so helpless.
I knew him when he was well,
able to do anything, full of energy …
When we were kids we played together
clambering in and out of boats, diving off the rocks,
giving cheek to the grown-ups, playing tricks,
running away …
And now he was disabled,
couldn't do any of those things: couldn't work, or play –
and was so humbly grateful to be carried from place to place.
As I took one corner of his bed,
using the strength in my arms and back,
I was thinking, 'God, suppose it was me,
lying here, would I be this patient?'
And when we got up on the roof,
and with busy hands removed the tiles and the rafters
and saw the plaster falling down
on the upturned, surprised faces
of the people inside the house:
I thought, 'This is like the tricks we used to play' –
and from his bed I heard him give the ghost of a laugh.

Third friend

Whatever happens, he's my friend.
I've known him for years but I don't really know what's wrong with him.
It is his body – but I think it's something in his mind, too.
It's as though he can't forgive himself for something –
and that makes him more ill.
In fact now he seems helpless, gripped by this guilt.
He sees himself as a person who can't do anything right.
Who can't do anything … who just can't …
and who isn't worth helping.
So at least we can show him we want to help;
surround him with our belief that he is worth it.

We can walk down the street at the four corners of his bed –
even if everyone is thinking 'What good will that do?'
We can refuse to be put off by the crowd –
even if they laugh or ignore us.
We can climb up the outside stairs to the roof –
even if they try to stop us.
We can break through the roof, and let the sun shine in,
and let our friend down gently, right at Jesus' feet.
And Jesus will see
that we believe in his help –
and we believe our friend is worth helping.

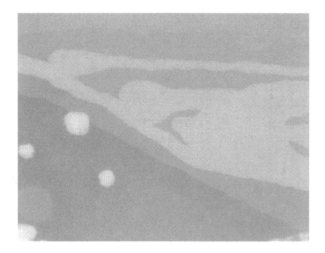

Fourth friend

I saw how angry they were:
angry with us for breaking in, angry with our friend,
for landing among them in a cloud of dust;
angry with Jesus, for what he said.
He told our friend, 'Your sins are forgiven.'
That surprised me, too –
anyone could see it was his legs that were the problem.
Though, in fact, Jesus was looking at us,
as much as our friend.

Four friends

What could he see –

looking up against the sun that streamed in –
except four people who believed in what they were doing,
and were open for whatever Jesus would do?
But those other people had closed minds.
They were ready to be angry with whatever Jesus did;
ranted that it was wrong to say his sins were forgiven.
Not an easy thing to say – but Jesus meant it.
It's not easy, either, to say, 'Stand up and walk.'
Jesus did both. That made them more angry!
So they stayed muttering in the dark house.
But we were overjoyed, because he did stand up,
and he did walk, out into the sunlight.
Here and now, seeing our friend made whole again,
we four know that this is God's work.

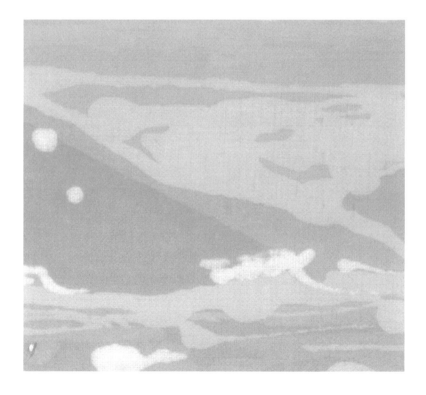

Four friends

The wind and the waves

(MARK 4:35–41)

The wind and the waves
that's what we notice –
the weather outside:
real wet rain, that defies our weatherproofs
and gets into our boots;
winds that stir things up,
blow us off course, cancel the ferries,
change our plans – real winds of change.
Weather that gives us
good news and bad … something to worry about …
plenty to talk about.

What else is out there beside the weather?
Other things that rock the boat
and shake our faith –
crises, controversies, news headlines –
of course we notice them too;
they are all around us, topical, tangible –
and, like the weather, beyond us.

Touching us more closely, but still outside our control,
there's disability, isolating us from the busy world;
the loss of those we love, cutting us adrift.
Now Jesus challenges us to look again
at what's going on inside each one of us –
in our minds, our hearts, our gut reactions,
our fears – and hopes
our anxieties – and our dreams.
'Why are you so afraid?'

What is it that moves us,
motivates or paralyses with dread?
Hurts or heals?
What enables us to sleep like a trusting child?
Or makes us cry for help in the darkness?
Why do we believe we can't cope
and then, at the heart of the storm, find courage
and a great calm?
'Where is your faith?'

God, help us to perceive your presence,
and to receive your peace –
more powerful than the storms outside,
healing the conflict within.
Let your calm bless our whole being,
may we become whole …

Amen

A man

(MATTHEW 7:9)

I am a man
whose son asked him for bread
and who gave him a stone.

Only joking.
Boys don't cry.
Don't want him to become soft.
Got to learn to fend for himself,
fight his corner,
learn to be a breadwinner.

He held the stone in his small hand.
He looked me in the eye.
The tears were there,
but they didn't fall.
Things were never the same again.

There was no bread between us.

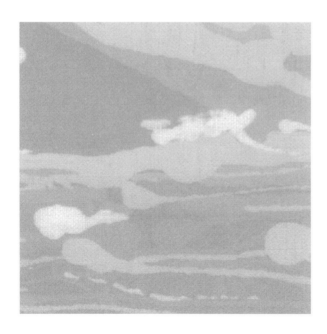

I am Jairus' daughter.
Everyone called me 'child'.
Suddenly I was so tired.
Not hungry. It hurt.
I lay on my bed between sleeping and waking.
And I went a long way away
so I could barely hear my parents calling.

Then I heard the people crying,
wailing and crying
and I smelled the bread baking
to feed them all.
But I was only hungry
to be touched.
I was so lonely,
lying there and leaving home
and it got darker.

And then a hand took hold of mine,
a warm and friendly hand
and I heard someone saying
'Get up, my child.'
So I sat up, blinking
because it was bright daylight.
Why was I in bed?
Why was the house full of people?
Why was my mother crying?

The man holding my hand said
'Give her something to eat.'
And they brought me bread
warm from the oven.
Now I was hungry.
My hands were trembling.

A child speaks

(LUKE 8:40–42, 49–55)

He helped me to break it,
floury on my lips,
salty on my tongue,
filling my belly –
such good bread.
I ate every last crumb.
It tasted of life.

A child speaks

In the presence of all the people

(LUKE 8:40, 42B–48)

In the presence of all the people,
a crowd – a whole bunch of individuals –
none completely whole –
who focused on Jesus, jostled to catch his words,
shushed and shuggled, pushed and surged forward,
trod on each other's toes …
A holy and unholy huddle
each aware only of his or her own needs,
powerful because of their numbers,
easily excluding the weak and those on the edge –
present then and there for all sorts of reasons.

In the presence of all the people –
that was the real challenge
for the woman …
Just by being there she broke the law
which defined her body as unclean.
Weakened by constant bleeding,
she still found the strength of purpose
and faith, empowering her to push through the crowd,
to get nearer to Jesus,
but believed that through touch, through her presence,
she passed on blood taint:
her pain was both in body and in spirit,
because she saw herself as the problem.
She took a great risk
in reaching out to Jesus
in the presence of all the people.

Right there,
in the presence of all the people,
Jesus suddenly felt power
go out of him: an emptiness.
A question: Who touched me?
Why ask! exclaim his friends:
Who isn't touching someone else in this press?

Who could possibly be aware
of one among many, of one heart beating wildly,
one reason for staying hidden,
one hand reaching out,
one slender thread of hope?
Who but Jesus, risking that awareness,
risking a meeting with the unseen person,
opening up acceptance and fullness of healing
in the presence of all the people …

The crowd, Jesus, the woman, wholly in the presence of God.

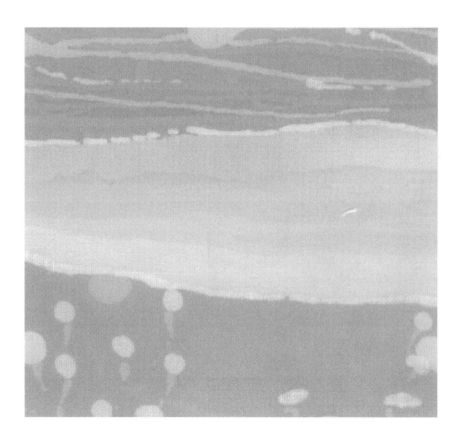

*In the presence of
all the people*

Two voices

(LUKE 8:40–56)

I was in the crowd.

> I was at home.

I had been ill for twelve years – women's problems.

> I was twelve years old, on the brink of womanhood.

I risked even entering a public place …
I was cut off from community, like one dead.

> I was ill – near death – going into a dark place
> where even my parents' love could not keep me safe.

I had no family. I had to fend for myself.

> I was at the heart of my family, and in their prayers,
> but my illness put me almost out of reach.

I reached out in the crowd.

> I was hidden in the home.

I was hidden in the crowd.
My bleeding made me unclean – I was untouchable.
But I was real and present
to Jesus who asked, 'Who touched me?'

> Those who loved me believed Jesus could heal me.
> But then they thought I was dead –
> so I should not be touched.
> But Jesus took my hand.

It was my own faith that made me whole.
I reached out in the crowd.

> Jesus took my hand.
> He said, 'Child, get up.'

He said, 'Who touched me?'
I trembled, and found the courage
to tell them all that I was healed.

> My spirit returned. I got up, I ate.
> My life began again.
> I went on growing up.

I went on my way in peace.

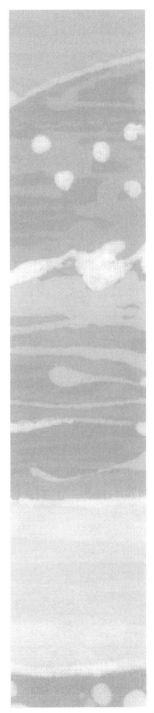

Salt

(MATT 5:13–16)

Salt!
Think salt –
taste it on your tongue –
imagine salt, be salt.
Get your mind round it,
get your lives round it.

Salt! Blessed salt:
blessing with a bite,
with a tang of the sea –
harvested from the waves,
or from barren plains,
or punishing salt-mines.

A precious commodity,
carried long distances on salt roads –
treasured and taxed and given pride of place at table.
Wars have been fought over it,
and many tears shed.

Salt, elemental –
essential to life,
down-to-earth chemistry.

Perfect crystals
ground down to be of service.
Making dye fast, glazing pots –
subtly colouring the world.

Salt – life-affirming,
bringing out the flavour of bread
and baked potatoes,
everyday food:
enhancing the joy of tasting.

But also needed
to keep food from wasting:
to preserve meat, fish from going rotten
to preserve health –
saving salt.

Salt that we sweat in our daily work,
in our fear;
tears that we shed.
Salt is emetic, too –
you can have too much of a good thing:
it is abrasive: scrubs, scours, purifies;
on snowy paths helps get a grip.
Salty ones – don't lose your grip!

You are salt.
You have a tang of goodness
a saving grace –
and a taste of salvation.

A voice in the street

(MATTHEW 15:21–28)

There's a voice in the street –
not singing but sobbing –
calling for help
for a child who is ill:
pleading with the powerful,
caring about the detail of human dignity,
hoping against reason –
calling out for healing.
Calling out for healing.

There's a voice in the street –
not sweetly reasonable
but shouting –
strident and resistant,
a voice not to be ignored,
calling out for justice, calling for change,
across a divide between two nations –
calling out for healing.
Calling out for healing.

There's a voice in the street –
that will not be silenced –
arguing with conviction:
a woman standing her ground
when a man does not listen
when he puts her down;
defying prejudice with courage,
defending the little ones with love,
restoring relationship with laughter –
calling out for healing.
Calling out for healing.

There are voices in the street –
not then and there
but here and now –
challenging the powers that be,
putting the case for the powerless,
in dialogue for reconciliation,
picking up the pieces, sharing the crumbs,
daring to speak
with courage, with laughter, with faith.

God hears those voices
and God is in those voices –
and there is healing.
And there is healing.

Some went up the mountain

(MATT 17:1–8, 14–16)

Some went up the mountain.

Some stayed on the plain.

A handful went with Jesus.

The others were left with a crowd gathering,
folk in an in-between time,
waiting for something to happen.

It took time to climb the mountain.
Those who scrambled up, among the barren rocks,
wondered what was waiting for them
on the mountain top.
They climbed so high they were hidden in the cloud,
as though they were out of this world.

Their friends were in the world, no question,
surrounded by down-to-earth problems,
face to face with the crowd:
the hungry, hurting, hopeful crowd,
reminding them of a whole world of suffering
where they felt helpless.

On the mountain top, Peter, James and John
were face to face with Jesus –
suddenly saw their friend in a different light.
His face shone like the sun;
his clothes were dazzling white.
He was not alone: Moses and Elijah,
heroes, leaders from another time,
seemed to stand alongside him.
The cloud that surrounded them was bright:
full of God's energy.

Down in the crowd came the cry of a frightened child,
light and darkness flashing before his eyes,
random energy let loose in his brain:
falling to the ground in a fit.
His father turned to the friends of Jesus for help.
They did not know where to turn.
They were afraid.

Those on the mountain were amazed.
God was telling them: 'This is my Son.'
In a moment that lasted for ever
they fell down on the ground –
in wonder, in terror.
But Jesus came close to them again,
lifted them up, said, 'Do not be afraid.'

Together, they came down the mountain –
into the crowd, into the here and now,
into the time of crisis,
the place where people struggle and are afraid.
They carried with them courage,
energy for the task,
a deeper faith, a new way of seeing Jesus.
And, within them, they carried the light
that shone from his face:
a light for those who waited on the plain,
bringing healing and hope.

Woman with ointment

(JOHN 12:1–11)

On my knees –
not, for once, scrubbing tiles
or coaxing wax from the chancel carpet;
not arranging flowers
but anointing feet.
By what authority?
Intuition, imagination and love.

On my knees –
time and time again:
tying shoelaces,
taking out splinters, counting toes:
is there space in the structures of the Church
for motherly care
and family jokes –
for intuition, imagination, love?

On my knees –
getting personal:
coming close, touching, taking risks
of being misunderstood;
filling the air with fragrance, spilling it,
massaging calloused skin,
stiff joints, weary flesh –
how dare I?
Through intuition, imagination, love.

On my knees –
where the poor and unnoticed always are:
shining shoes, searching in the gutter,
picking up crumbs.

Right there, on the bottom line,
you will find me, having spent all I had
on this one thing, now pouring it out
extravagantly –
out of intuition, imagination, love.

On my knees –
doing something at once symbolic and down-to-earth,
about responsibility, respect
and remembering;
about life and death, ends and beginnings.
A representative person
who is also a human being
in a particular time and place:
frail, fallible, gifted
with intuition, imagination, love.

On my knees –
when I'm down here
actions speak louder than words.
But so low (grassroots, shop floor, street level)
you cannot hear my voice;
and when you put me on a pedestal
you cannot see my face.
If we meet somewhere in the middle,
on common ground,
we can serve each other
and rise together –
sharing intuition, imagination, love.

Why this waste?

(MARK 14:1–9)

Why this waste?
and why is Jesus behaving as though it is all right –
putting us in the wrong?
What is this woman doing here?
Choosing to use all her resources
in a way that challenges us:
acting with such authority –
like a priest anointing a king –
by what right?
She's just a woman, after all.
A woman – how dare she –
doing such a touchy-feely thing
to the one we follow, and respect,
and don't always understand –
as though she knows, intuitively,
his hopes, his fears, and his deepest need.

Why is Jesus weeping?
Is he weeping for Jerusalem?
Is he weeping for himself?
Is he weeping for us?
Is he shedding the tears we hold back?
Why does this make us afraid?

What does it mean – to be handed over?
To stand between two policemen
to be cautioned, charged,
photographed, numbered,
fingerprinted, filed,
locked up;

to be stripped of possessions,
to become 'the prisoner',
and to be rendered powerless, nameless,
passive
as a body under the surgeon's knife.
To wait on the decisions of others,
to be set aside, subjected,
to lose control of your life …
What does it mean to be handed over ?
– to be crucified?

How dare she prepare his body for burial?
We cannot cope without him.
We cannot face his being handed over.
Where is the good news in all this?
Why this waste?
O God why this waste?

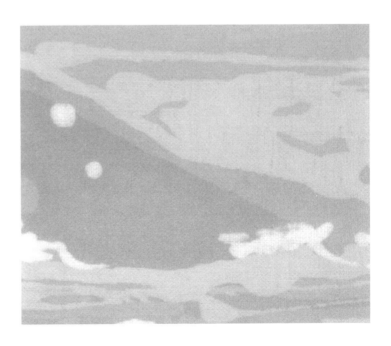

Words from the Cross

(JOHN 19: 30B)

Jesus said, 'It is finished.'
Then he bowed his head and gave up his spirit.

This is the end
and we will all come to it.
We are mortal. Our bodies wear out,
cannot stand the strain and shock
of the world in which we live as mortal beings.
In Jesus, God entered our mortality,
crept into this fragile shell
which is unique, beautiful, but not eternal.
We exist in time.
Jesus lived in a particular time and place,
and died at a moment of time.
as each of us will do.

But how he died!
He died alone
and yet with all eyes on him
in anguish, in terror,
in love, in despair.
We cannot know what was in his mind
any more than the figures falling –
arms outstretched through space –
from the burning tower
on a day we can never forget.
A day fixed in time.

But we remember now
that there was another moment in time
after which nothing would ever be the same:
when the man Jesus cried, 'It is finished'
and fell out of the world.
Out of time.
Leaving a great emptiness
and silence.

Jesus said, 'It is finished.'
Then he bowed his head and gave up his spirit.

This is the day
Six reflections

What did Jesus do on the Sabbath?

How did he make a difference to the lives of ordinary men and women?

What difference does that make to us today?

Here and now

(Luke 4:16–21)

Here and now
at a point in history,
a place in our story,
in his home town,
in our local synagogue,
on an ordinary Sabbath
among us, his neighbours,
he opened the book
and read, for all to hear,
words of extraordinary promise.
> And we said 'Yes!
> Those are the words we like to hear.
> Yes, Lord! Amen!'

Here and now
he told us what the words meant –
they filled us with hope
but also unsettled us,
because they are not about
any other place,
or any other people,
not to do with the distant past
or the faint future.
But are God's extraordinary challenge
to us, ordinary people,
here and now.
'Today, in your hearing, these words have come true.'
> And we said 'No, no –
> this is not what we want to hear!'
> And we chased him out of town.

But his words still hang in the air
and those words are still there,

on the scroll in the synagogue,
visited on the Sabbath,
but written on our hearts
every day of the week –
words for ordinary people
of extraordinary hope and challenge.
Whether we say yes or no
the words are coming home …
the words have found their time …
here and now.

Here and now

The disciples

(*LUKE 6:1–5*)

We are the disciples:
when we were boys
we scrumped apples,
ate them and threw away the cores.
Now we walk through the fields,
plucking ears of corn,
rubbing them between our palms
and eating the milky, floury kernels.

'Stop that!' shouted the Pharisees
'Don't you know it's the Sabbath –
how dare you
reap the corn and winnow it?
Next thing we know
you'll be baking it and setting up shop.
Keep the Sabbath holy!'

Jesus said 'But they're hungry.
Remember what the Bible says
about great King David:
when his men were starving
he took bread
from the house of God –
the bread offered to God,
the bread that only priests could eat –
and he shared it out
among ordinary people in their need.
What makes the Sabbath holy
is that we do good things on it.
What makes bread blessed
is the sharing.'

We listen to the argument –
all ears, licking our lips –
still savouring the grains of wheat,
free for all,
which were bread in the making,
daily bread
given to us, and God.

The disciples

Body language
(Luke 13:10–17)

You never noticed me,
except as a person in a pew,
never looked me in the face.
Though that would have been hard
for I always sat at the back,
huddled into the Methodist crouch,
doubled up in private devotion –
      or ducking
to avoid the blows of daily life.
I was in every way
a private person –
though you took it for dullness –
and as soon as worship ended
I scuttled away, before
your bland greeting at the door
could hazard a guess at my name.

Such upstanding Christians,
so sure of where you stood,
I couldn't hold up my head among you.

So returned home –
to a private place but in no way safe –
to violence, rejection, loneliness and shame.

You had prayed for me under several heads
but didn't recognise me in the flesh.

Sunday left me hungry for a meaning,
asking – 'What have I done wrong?
Is this the way it was meant to be?
How much more can I bear?
Why does God let this happen to me?
Does anyone care?'

My whole body
was a question mark –
and you never noticed.

This is the day

(LUKE 13:10–17)

This is the day,
this is the day
when he spoke the word
and touched my life,
when I stood up straight
and things became whole.

That for me is why
this day is different
from all other days.

You say it could have happened –
you say it should have happened –
on an ordinary working day.
'Come and be cured on one of them.
Come during surgery hours.
Why expect special treatment?'

But what happened
that Sabbath day,
made me see myself,
an ordinary person, as special –
and it set me free
from the treadmill of keeping going,
keeping going
from day to day.

After so many years,
I'd found a way
to live bent double.
Life was weighing me down,
but life had to go on.

So my horizons narrowed
to the earth
just under my feet –

like an ox or ass in a gingan
I went round and round,
bound to the tasks I could do.
I never looked anyone in the eye –
but I was coping.

For eighteen years –
and for six days of the week –
that was my life.

And on the seventh day,
in God's time,
I came to the synagogue.
My feet brought me.
And I could only look at my feet.
I could only look at all their feet.
I could only look at his feet.

But Jesus could see the whole of me.

He saw I was no beast of burden
but a child of God.
He said, 'You are rid of your trouble …'
He laid hands on me –
then and there he set me free.

And I straightened up –
I looked him straight in the eye,
I saw the whole earth and the encircling sky,
and I began to praise God.

And I still praise God –
who has given six days for work,
and one for ordinary people
to become special
and to be set free.

I am the man
who had the withered arm.
It hung limp and useless at my side.
It was my right arm, so I was useless too –
unhandy, a waste of space.
All the skills I'd learned
(I was a carpenter)
mocked me after my illness.
The best part of me was put on the shelf
with the tools of my trade.
I know that folk pitied me and my family –
with no breadwinner.
I was on the edge, disabled,
disempowered,
a non-person …
I stayed away
from the workshop, the quayside,
the market place,
the working world where other folk
bustled and bantered, purposeful, creative,
making a living six days of the week.
I had no part in it.

But I went to the synagogue
on the Sabbath day:
a day of rest – that's ripe
for someone who's unemployed.

And there and then
Jesus found a job for me –
he made me a visual aid!

I would have resented that –
but I knew it wasn't Jesus
who started this game.
I was pushed to the front of the crowd.

A man in the crowd
(MARK 3:1–6)

89

They were watching
to see whether Jesus would heal me.
They didn't ask me
what I wanted to happen.
I was a pawn in their game –
a statistic in their calculations.

Jesus called me out,
stood me in the middle.
Everything was quiet.
Everyone was looking at me,
at my useless arm.
I felt I was withering away
under their stares.
On the day the world was made,
God saw that it was good.
I thought they were seeing all the bad in me –
a person who could make nothing,
a wasted life.
Jesus asked was it right
to do good or evil
on the Sabbath,
to save life or kill?
They were silent.
I could have told him –
I could have told them all –
but my part was to stand there
like a wooden post, to be a sign.

*A man in
the crowd*

Then Jesus said
'Stretch out your hand.'
It wasn't an order, but an invitation.

I had a job to respond.
My arm had a mind of its own –
one long Sabbath rest.
But I willed wasted muscles
to do their best
And slowly I lifted it and stretched it out.
I put my hand into his hands –
and I got it back in working order.
I flexed the muscles,
waggled my fingers,
clenched a fist, punched the air –
knowing I was healed.

And so did they –
a gasp ran round the crowd.
How could he? How dare he?
In the synagogue! On the Sabbath!

They had made their point
and so had Jesus –
but the points were poles apart:
bad news and good news
at the same time.

And no one asked me
what it meant to me.
What do you think it meant?
Come and see.
But don't call me
'the man with the withered arm'
any more –
I'm back to work.

*A man in
the crowd*

You'll find me in the workshop,
on the quayside,
in the market place.
You'll see what I can do.
You'll hear me telling the world
about the work of my hands
that earns our daily bread
all through the week.
I know that what I do is good –
my yoke is easy,
my burden is light.

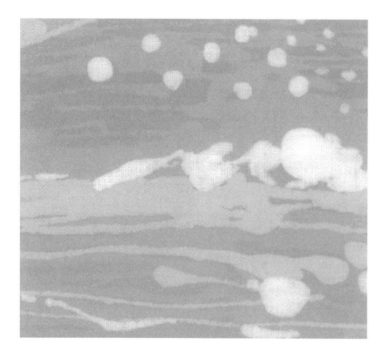

*A man in
the crowd*

Holy Saturday

(MARK 15:40–16:2)

Here we are
in the waiting room: the place
where everyone is a stranger; the space
between death and burial.

Numbness and
no-man's land.

We women kept watch
while Joseph from Arimathaea
went to ask for the body.
He has become an undertaker –
the borrowed tomb
a chapel of rest –
because now we are entering
a day of rest,
when even this task,
this last loving ministry,
must be left half-done.

Mourning is put on hold.

Death is a hard fact –
but somehow we need to touch it
one more time, to know
its finality, to show
our respect, to let go.

Meanwhile the story is incomplete.

We, the women, go on watching,
waiting for the Sabbath to be over,
so that we can return

with spices, at dawn
on the first day of the week –
and know for sure

it is finished:
the one we love is not there …
know there's nothing to wait for any more.

Holy Saturday

A. Leaping and singing he was,
   laughing and praising God!
   He was dancing – in the Temple –
   and everyone was amazed.
   But it was no more amazing
   than what had happened a few moments before:
   what we had done – dared to do – in Jesus' name.

B. At a precise time – three o'clock in the afternoon –
   in a precise place, at the gate called Beautiful,
   I was waiting – as I had been waiting all my life –
   for passers-by to throw me a coin,
   or, more likely, to step over me.
   That was the only place I expected to be –
   on the doorstep, on the edge, an outsider.
   That was the only way I expected to be –
   on the cadge, on the dole, on the receiving end.
   'Look,' said a voice, and I looked
   and I saw two ordinary men.

A. Ordinary uneducated men – myself and John –
   just two companions of Jesus. Without Jesus.
   The lame beggar looked at us,
   looked for a hand-out,
   and we had nothing to give. No money
   not even good advice. Just …

B. And he said, 'I have no silver or gold,
   but what I have I give you.'

A. I took this huge risk.
   I said, 'In the name of Jesus Christ of Nazareth
   stand up and walk.'

Leaping and singing

(Acts 3:1–10)

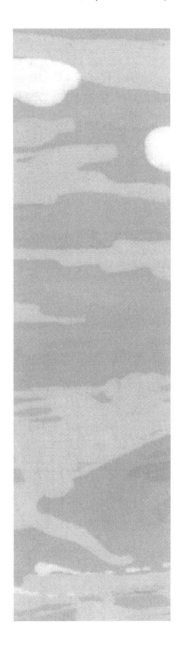

B. I had so much to lose.

A. I had so much to lose.
What if I was wrong? Was it possible?
There was no way I had the power or piety
to make this man walk.

B. What if he was wrong?
If I believed – and nothing happened?
I took this huge risk.
And he took me by the hand and raised me up.
My feet were strong … my ankles were strong,
my knees were strong … my feet began to dance.
I was praising God with my whole body.

A. We walked into the Temple – outsiders going in.

B. I danced into the Temple – my world turned upside down.

A. Ordinary people
in whom something amazing was happening –
through taking risks
in Jesus' name. Amen

Leaping and singing

Show us the river of the water of life,
crystal clear – as clear as the calm waters around Iona.
But not salt –
unless with honest sweat or healing tears.
Show us the river of the water of life,
and let us wade in the water:
first with cupped hands
quenching our thirst;
then wading deeper
to be washed clean, to be blessed.

Show us the river of the water of life
where the old order passes away –
is water under the bridge –
where there is no more pollution or drought,
where the face of our suffering world,
smudged with blood and grime and tears,
can be washed clean.

Show us the river of the water of life:
may we immerse ourselves in it,
be carried out of our depth
by the currents of your love –
abandoning ourselves into your hands,
being healed
and made whole.

And show us the trees of life –
the green and growing trees,
with deep roots in the flowing water,
with branches freely embracing the sky –
fruitful all year round:
part of creation and creative,
with fruits that delight
and with leaves that heal.

The river and the trees

(REV 22:1,2 AND PSALM 1)

Then show us how to be, ourselves,
like trees planted by the waterside:
part of creation, amid destruction;
and creative beings, amid discord;
where there is division, diverse;
beautiful in your eyes, as we become whole.
Unfolding leaves, fragile, translucent,
veined with living water, green with hope:
leaves that make a difference –
leaves for the healing of the nations.

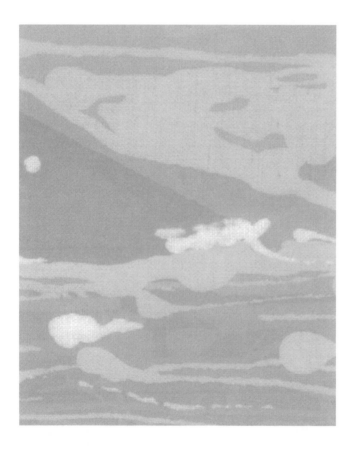

*The river
and the trees*

The Word in the world

– three sequences from beyond Iona –

Hospital poems
May 2002

Fever

All night long
my mind swung
through the branches
of the dream forest –
full of colour
and danger, voices
and intertwining meanings,
while gaudy birds
flew off in all directions.

Now the light
of a hospital dawn
flows gently into the ward
like the tide filling an estuary

and the grey herons
of reason and moderation
are watching, patient.

Warden in Ward B

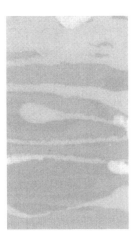

What foolishness brought me here –
what insurrection of bacteria?
Do I have the patience to become a patient –
or is this time-out timely, heaven-sent?
Should I meditate, moralise –
or just lie back and institutionalise?

The radio in the corner

'Every night you make my daydreams.'

Easy listening
becomes hard
when it's no one's choice, particularly.
Sunday slipping into evening in Ward B
sees an ugly litter of noise
strewn along the verges of lives
which are at the same time
pedestrian, dead ordinary
and steering a course, precariously,
between life and death.
Easy listening
becomes hard
when this is no one's choice.

Off centre

The centre
keeps pulling you back
so the loop shortens.
The turn of phrase, the stories
become more familiar
but still take you by surprise
and have the power
to delight you, or distress.

'It's much appreciated'
you say, 'but you see
I have Alzheimer's – I prefer not to say "disease" –
and it's all getting lost in there' …
pointing to the centre of your being.

'I'm forgetting so much …
I'm getting lost.'

And the tears come
as you tell again
the story of a lost child …
'But your kindness is much appreciated.'
And as I move away
to the edges of your world
I see you sit tight, wondering
what will wander off next
and whether the words can be found
to capture it again.

The centre
keeps pulling you back.
The loop shortens,
turns of phrase, stories
become more familiar –
but not less important.

It would be melodramatic
to call what is happening
a vortex,
but I admire your frail courage
in its face
and take it as a compliment –
maybe a blessing –
when you call me, to your visitors,
'an eccentric'.

It is much appreciated

Still life

Lit from the north
the day room's a neutral space:
pictures of lochs and steam boats,
posters reminding folk they should not smoke,
ill-at-easy chairs,
a potted plant, well watered –
without the febrile colours and decay
of bedside bouquets –
a safe and soothing green.

Catching the window light
a tray of fragile china cups,
a pot of tea gone cold –
for those who waited
through the night
and, now daylight has come,
have nothing to wait for
and are still alive.

Hospital poems

Faslane 2002

Singing across Mull

Feeling small, insignificant, powerless, alone
I sing as I travel into the unknown.
How many others have raised fearful faces
and reedy voices, among these glens –
or in darker places?
How many, doing so, have raised their hearts
when hope seemed dead and gone?
And, through song alone,
found strength to travel on?

Kathy and Molly

Ministers without collars
or churches –
I hear one of you liberating song
against the barbed wire,
and watch the other feeding people in detention
the bread rolls you buttered and filled before dawn –
enough for all including the police.
Where such ministry is happening
who needs church order?

Clergy action

The congregation have voted in favour
of Justice and Peace (like Motherhood and apple pie)
However, some members are critical
of a minister who protests
or may even be arrested early in the morning:
this is not respectable
(unlike Motherhood)
or tasteful (unlike apple pie).
You are cheerfully unrepentant
about 'what I choose to do on my day off'.

Come to think of it, was God being respectable,
early in the morning
on Easter Sunday?

At the gates

We shared Communion at the gates of Faslane:
one of the places in a broken world
where breaking bread and drinking bitter wine
is most relevant.
We shared it to remember
security – not of barbed wire and missiles –
but of God's love
that risks all and gives life.
We shared, in a warm circle of believers.
But later, when we sat down on the cold road,
we found that the bread and the cup
had escaped, and were still out there in the crowd,
being shared, carefully, among people of all kinds:
this paradox
of pain and promise
being passed from hand to hand
in a broken world.

On the line

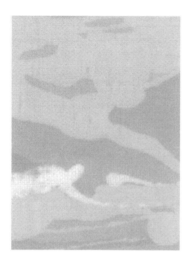

Quietness flows back
on the edge of the crowd.
Hills are still there
and the impartial clouds.
Drumbeats and shouting distanced.

I stand in line waiting to be charged,
and, between formal words
and human conversation,
find the silence I need
to observe the tracery of twigs,
with buds ready to break
on both sides of the wire.

Policewomen at Clydebank

I don't know your names
but I will remember your laughter,
our conversation,
your uncompromised humanity.
There was respect between all of us
in that waiting room,
where some of us were detained
and others only doing their job.
Being human together –
this is what keeps us alive
and makes life worth living.

Faslane 2002

Office

First the fingertips of my left hand,
rolled one by one
to make patterned squares, each one different;
then the side of my hand
then the palm
then one whole fingerprint
(how I thought it would be);
then repeat with the right hand
meticulously.
Viscous black ink rolled out on a metal plate
as though for a lino cut,
fine white paper smoothed
like a communion cloth:
these are the rituals I know –
of creativity and sacrament.
The young police officer is intent
on her craft, not officious, but careful
of people and prints:
explaining as she goes,
getting it right.
I wonder what different exchanges
this room has seen –
anger, fear, rights demanded
and denied. Resistant hands,
ink smudged across the page.
Realising that I too have no right to say no,
there is still part of me
that stands quietly in this room
observing another person doing a job,
aware of a mystery
and watching the unique and intricate beauty
of my prints unfold.

Faslane 2002

Cell

Three women sleep in a cell
on a cold floor
enclosed by cold bare walls.
Three people who, sometime, could share
stories of warmth, nourishment,
laughter of living, hope of new life
and the commitment
that brought them to this place.
But now we are too tired, worn with wanting change.
Also with cold that creeps into our bones
and into our soul.

Crumbs

These are just crumbs of discomfort.
In other parts of the world
people are detained without trial,
tortured, kept in solitary, starved,
deprived of human rights.
Here, people with different lives
grow up in institutions, become persistent offenders,
are brutalised, never know their birthright.
So, having been read our rights
are we just playing
at being part of this broken world
or do these crumbs we taste
contain the whole world
for which we pray
and, mysteriously, the way God enters it?

Faslane 2002

Time

In the police station
time is arrested.
Not only do they take away, as instructed, watches and diaries,
but inside, without windows, sound deadened,
you lose all sense of the moving world,
people on the street, mundane traffic,
and, further out,
hillside burns, water under bridges,
children's impatient feet,
tide's ebb and flow,
the time it takes a cloud to cross the sky,
the time it takes a tree to grow.

Time is measured instead
by the beating of your heart,

a face in the door offering water,

the darkening of the skylight,

voices approaching,

the turn of a key.

Hospitality
(For Norman and Ruth)

When I came to your door
confused after losing a day
you gave me time:
time to talk, time to listen
time to put food on the table
time to eat, time to sleep
and the time hidden
in a hyacinth still to flower
another day.

Faslane 2002

Meanwhile, the mouse

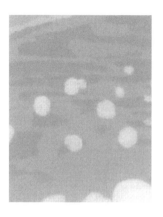

Anna
there might just be a connection
between the mouse
caught in our humane trap in the kitchen
and your mother gently detained in Clydebank –
both a whisker away
from the pain of the real world.

Prayer

On alien ground, absurd,
afraid, humiliated, put to the test,
I was lost for words.
Next day, on the way home,
remembered the taste of humanity,
and found my tongue.

Living Word – thank you for setting me free
through pain and poetry.
You are good news in the present tense,
changing the world; you are profound
meaning given a common sense.
In you, peace becomes possibility
as we together find the common ground.

Faslane 2002

110

Thembi's house

(Habitat for Humanity 'Blitzbuild', Orange Farm, Soweto, South Africa, 3–7 February 1999. I took part in this immediately before coming to work on Iona. It was a preparation – and a privilege.)

The foundations are already down.
It is still early in the day,
but the sun is hot
on the dusty rectangle
like a threshing floor,
like a dancing floor.

We stand around like wallflowers
waiting for the dance to begin –
waiting to be drawn in.

Partners possibly,
tentatively
looking each other in the eye,
greeting each other
with a threefold handshake.

Thembi, hoping to move
from the shack on this site
to the house which is still
only an idea in our minds;

her sisters, willing to help;
Samuel, the builder,
Sandra, the bricklayer –
who know how it can be done;
Meshach and Rachel,
Jan and Ephraim, the volunteers.

Empty-handed – but not for long.

We form a human chain
to pass concrete blocks
across the beaten earth
over the threshold
into the working space –
and before we know where we are
the dance has begun.

We're mixing the first mortar
(yellow sand, river sand
and cement) with water,
carried from the standpipe outside the gate:
turning and churning
with heavy spades
then hefting it
to where the bricklayers have begun work.

Sandra and Samuel spread it thick and swift
with the pointed trowel;
each block is slapped down,
checked against the line,
tamped into place,
oozing mortar scraped up
with a flick of the wrist
and packed into the gaps –
and the next
and the next.

The sun climbs higher in the sky
and the walls begin to rise,
first one course,
then another.

Thembi's house

We break, gratefully,
there is tea from a kettle
doorsteps of bread and jam:

toasted by the sun
we seek the small shade of Thembi's yard –
sapling fig tree and peach.

Then more sun, dust, blocks,
more mortar!
Sweating, lifting
mixing and carrying
in the heat of the day.
And the blessing of water
gushing from the tap set crooked
on a standpipe hot to the touch,
water cooling hands, face,
quenching the thirst
of children
trudging home from school –
water, too precious to waste.

In the long afternoon
the pace slows.
There is laughter, and banter
as we wash our hands at the tap
and sit on dusty ground
to eat mealie meal porridge
and cabbage stew
from Thembi's dusky kitchen.

Then back to work,
circling the growing walls,
till evening falls
and we go back through the township,
to wash, and stretch out and sleep.

Rising with the sun
at cock-crow, dog-bark, child-voice;
breakfast of tea and bread;

*Thembi's
house*

a walk through the red dust
to the common ground
we found on the first day.

Now there is no water in the tap
to mix the mortar –
no water in the township.
Women wait with buckets and drums.

While we wait, there's time
to see all the care that's gone
into this place.
'Shanty town' barely does it justice.
Where each plot is fenced off, beans grow up the wire mesh,
enclosing grass plots,
fruit trees and shade trees,
tomatoes, corn, sunflowers.
The bare earth before each door
is neatly swept.
Each home is different, huts
of scavenged tin and timber,
broken blocks, plywood,
fragments of hoardings advertising a different world.
Each has curtains drawn
against the sun
and the curious strangers busy in the shell
of a home yet to become.

The tap spits, sneezes,
and with the water flowing,
we begin again –
mixing, lifting, carrying,
sweating, laying bricks,
as the sun leaps up in the sky
like the lord of the dance.
All day we tread its measures

Thembi's house

weary but unwilling to end,
until the walls are higher than our heads
and the windows gape for their glass
and the roof timbers are ready to be raised –
morning to evening, another day,
another good day.

By the fourth day –
after setbacks and near-disaster –
the roof-trusses point to the sky
like praying hands.
We greet each other again
with a triple handshake
and the grins of old friends.
We call each other by name –
and cannot wait
to begin the next figure of the dance.

The sun leads us out
onto the floor
and the hammers of the carpenters
beat a rhythm all day,
while dried mortar is smoothed down
and the walls backwashed.
Hands work putty
and carefully set panes of glass in place;
brand new corrugated iron roof panels
come marching out, one by one,
shining in the sun
under which (pacing ourselves now)
we weave in and out
with steps which have become second nature.

Wide-eyed children wander by
watching grown-ups
learning through play;

Thembi's house

witnessing a home
believed into being.

Until – sweaty, dirty,
thirsty and aching –
we slacken our pace.
Evening is coming,
the sun's boldness is gone,
fear of darkness and disorder
sends the workers on their way.
Thembi calls her children home.

It is the last day.
Early sun blesses the township,
gilding grasses, glinting on tin roofs,
as beautiful and full of possibility
as the first day –
when God saw that all was good.

This Sunday cannot be a day of rest.

This is the last lap.
As the builders gather
the sun is already baking the earth,
and again there is no water in the tap.
But the work goes on, step by step:

Thembi and her sisters making
a strong statement of paint
on the outer walls.
Inside, the last high course
of bricks to be laid,
the gaps to be filled,
the armadillo of roof sheets
to be lifted into place –
clangour of hammers on metal hour after hour

*Thembi's
house*

while sun resonates in the sky
like a great cymbal.

Men astride the roof look out
like kings or conquerors
over square miles of human life –
a shimmering landscape
of mirage and paradox.
But here there's shade
and common sense –
in the shelter of a roof.

Mouths are dry
because there is no water in the tap,
and drier still, as women with brooms
sweep the concrete floor
free of the dust and rubble of four days' work.
A cup of cool water
passed from hand to hand
is a sacrament.
Co-workers, sharing
moments of frustration and fulfilment –
sharing laughter –
strangers who have become
dancing partners.

Nearly time to call the house complete
and we discover
that the threshold is too high
and we cannot hang the door –
to which, with great ceremony,
Thembi will be given the key.

Too late to worry now –
the guests are on their way:
builders of other homes (twenty five in five days)

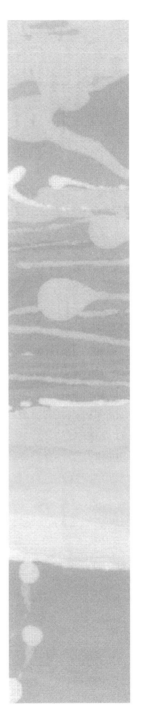

Thembi's house

corporate sponsors (less dusty, amazingly uncrumpled)
the neighbours (full of good-natured curiosity)
gathering to celebrate
good fortune and hard work.
So we stop hammering, sweeping, worrying
and let the speeches begin.

Under the bright-as-a-Sunday-penny sun
Thembi keeps an open house.
From the coolness
of the space we have created –
a human space
between strong walls –
from under the shelter of a roof,
singing is welling out like living water.

So come through the open door,
come in and join the throng
of neighbours and householders,
craftsmen and women and volunteers,
greeting each other
with a threefold handshake,
calling each other by name,
singing praise to God
and dancing –
with bare feet
and working boots
and Sunday best shoes –
dancing with five days of creation to celebrate –
dancing to the music of common humanity
on common ground.

*Thembi's
house*

Using the biblical reflections

The material in the biblical reflections section was written to be used as part of the Ministry of the Word during worship in the Abbey or Michael Chapel on Iona, or sometimes during programme sessions, or even on the weekly pilgrimage around the island. The words are themselves small pilgrimages, explorations of scripture, risky journeys encouraged by the Spirit, not always with a sure outcome. They are not expositions of scripture, but one way of understanding the passages: a way which may raise questions or begin new journeys for others. They can be used for private reflection, but were mostly written to be shared by folk worshipping together.

Some are monologues (*A man, A child speaks, Woman with ointment*). Others need more than one voice. In *Four friends*, we listen to four witnesses, four separate statements. In *Leaping and singing*, two voices alternate, and the 'parts' are marked A and B. The piece would not work with a single voice, and clearly it would help if they were distinctively different. This is even more the case with *Two voices*. Ideally one would be that of a child or teenager, one an older woman. *Some went up the mountain* looks at a Gospel story from the viewpoint of two groups of disciples: those who witnessed the transfiguration, and those who struggled with a pastoral situation at the foot of the mountain. Two voices, or even two groups of speakers, could be used here, alternating as shown by the layout.

A voice in the street calls for a response: from other members of the worship team, or indeed from the whole congregation, if the piece is printed out. With others the response could be sung: e.g. a chant such as *Ubi caritas* (Taizé) sung between sections of a reading such as *Woman with ointment*, or a *Kyrie* interwoven with *In the presence of all the people*. A familiar hymn could be used similarly. For instance *For the Healing of the nations* (Fred Kaan) could be used with *The river and the trees*: with two verses sung at the beginning, then the reflection read by one or more voices, then the whole congregation singing the last two verses of the hymn. *While shepherds watched their flocks by night* could be introduced by a reading of *Angels and shepherds*. There are many such creative variations, for which I invite you to draw on the musical repertoire of your congregation. In one case, a particular folk hymn, *'This is the day that the Lord has made … we will rejoice and be glad in it'* inspired a whole sequence: *This is the day*. It was used as part of a programme, rather than an act of worship, which included times for discussion, silent reflection and creative writing. The repeated song held the whole together. It would be relevant used with any of the readings – e.g. *A man in the crowd* – used on its own. As it happens, that monologue also links with Tom Colvin's African song *Christ the Worker*.

The two reflections based on Luke 13:10–17 can be used very effectively together, but need a space between them, which could be provided by instrumental music. Worship leaders will be able to identify other readings where music can provide space for reflection. 'Sound effects' can also add drama – e.g. the singing bowl in *The Word*, a rattle in *The tempter*.

But the words and images here can simply be used, in solitary reflection or read clearly aloud, to take us on a journey, and bring us back to the beautiful, ambiguous, challenging words of the Bible.

The Abbey: a prayer

Thank God for this place of meeting,
may it be a welcoming place,
a shelter-house
against the cold winds and the storms of life.

This stone barn, storing harvests of history,
be also God's place
an open space
where lives can be shaken out
and turned upside down:
space for finding ourselves face to face.

Approached at pilgrimage pace:
first a homecoming
then a centring –
time out, in God's time –
then a sending place.

A safe space
and a thin place:
common ground
and holy ground.

Amen

The Iona Community

The Iona Community, founded in 1938 by the Revd George MacLeod, then a parish minister in Glasgow, is an ecumenical Christian community committed to seeking new ways of living the Gospel in today's world. Initially working to restore part of the medieval abbey on Iona, the Community today remains committed to 'rebuilding the common life' through working for social and political change, striving for the renewal of the church with an ecumenical emphasis, and exploring new, more inclusive approaches to worship, all based on an integrated understanding of spirituality.

The Community now has over 240 Members, about 1500 Associate Members and around 1500 Friends. The Members – women and men from many denominations and backgrounds (lay and ordained), living throughout Britain with a few overseas – are committed to a fivefold Rule of devotional discipline, sharing and accounting for use of time and money, regular meeting, and action for justice and peace.

At the Community's three residential centres – the Abbey and the MacLeod Centre on Iona, and Camas Adventure Camp on the Ross of Mull – guests are welcomed from March to October and over Christmas. Hospitality is provided for over 110 people, along with a unique opportunity, usually through week-long programmes, to extend horizons and forge relationships through sharing an experience of the common life in worship, work, discussion and relaxation. The Community's shop on Iona, just outside the Abbey grounds, carries an attractive range of books and craft goods.

The Community's administrative headquarters are in Glasgow, which also serves as a base for its work with young people, the Wild Goose Resource Group working in the field of worship, a bi-monthly magazine, *Coracle*, and a publishing house, Wild Goose Publications.

For information on the Iona Community contact:
The Iona Community, Fourth Floor, Savoy House, 140 Sauchiehall Street,
Glasgow G2 3DH, UK. Phone: 0141 332 6343
e-mail: ionacomm@gla.iona.org.uk; web: www.iona.org.uk

For enquiries about visiting Iona, please contact:
Iona Abbey, Isle of Iona, Argyll PA76 6SN, UK. Phone: 01681 700404
e-mail: ionacomm@iona.org.uk

Dandelions and Thistles
Biblical meditations from the Iona Community
Jan Sutch Pickard (ed)

A beautiful illustrated book presenting Bible stories in the form of radical, thought-provoking meditations by various contributors. These monologues, scripts and poems give profound and sensitive messages in a simple and direct style accessible to all, making them perfect for use in group or worship situations or for individual reflection.

Contributors include: Jan Sutch Pickard, Kate McIlhagga, John L. Bell, Joy Mead, Ruth Burgess, Yvonne Morland, David Osborne, Kathy Galloway, Norman Shanks, John Davies, Anna Briggs.

96 pp   ISBN 1 901557 14 6

Advent Readings from Iona
Brian Woodcock and Jan Sutch Pickard

Christ of the cosmos, living Word,
come to heal and save ...
Incognito, in our streets,
beneath the concrete,
between the cracks,
behind the curtain, within the dreams,
in ageing memories, in childhood wonder,
in secret ponds, in broken hearts,
in Bethlehem stable, still small voice,
Word of God, amongst us.

Celebrate Christmas with reflections and prayers for each day of Advent. This effective antidote to the commercialism of the festive season can be used for individual meditation or group worship.

96 pp   ISBN 1 901557 33 2

Iona Abbey Worship Book
Liturgies and worship material used in Iona Abbey

Services and resources reflecting the Iona Community's commitment to the belief that worship is all that we are and all that we do, both inside and outside the church, with no division into the 'sacred' and the 'secular'. A companion songbook is also available.

272 pp   ISBN 1 901557 50 2   *Songbook:* 160 pp   ISBN 1 901557 73 1

These and more can be ordered from www.ionabooks.com